Y0-AGK-023

The Basketball Shooting Guide

by Sidney Goldstein

author of **The Basketball Coach's Bible**

and **The Basketball Player's Bible**

GOLDEN AURA PUBLISHING

The Nitty-Gritty Basketball Series

The Basketball Shooting Guide
by Sidney Goldstein

Published by:

GOLDEN AURA PUBLISHING

Post Office Box 41012

Philadelphia, PA 19127 U.S.A.

All rights reserved. No part of this book may be reproduced or transmitted to any form or by any means without written permission from the author.

Ist Edition Copyright © 1994 by Sidney Goldstein
2nd Edition Copyright © 1999 by Sidney Goldstein

Second printing Feb 1997
Third Printing Jan 2003

Printed in the U.S.A.

Library of Congress Catalog Card Number: 94-96502

Goldstein, Sidney

The Basketball Shooting Guide / Sidney Goldstein.--1st ed.

Basketball-Coaching

ISBN 1-884357-30-X

Softcover

Contents

Introduction

Over many years of coaching, planning, and studying, I found ways to teach each and every skill even to the most unskilled player. This scheme of learning did not come from any book. I tried things in practice. I modified them till they worked. Even players who could not simultaneously chew bubble gum and walk learned the skills. This booklet, part of **The Nitty-Gritty Basketball Series**, is one result of this effort. I believe you can benefit from my work.

Who Can Use This Information

This booklet is the perfect tool for anybody who wants to coach, teach, and/or learn basketball:

- A parent who wants to teach his or her child
- A player who wants to understand and play the game better
- A little league or recreation league coach
- A high school or junior high school coach
- A college coach, a professional coach
- A women's or a men's coach

This booklet contains material from **The Basketball Player's Bible**. Chapter 1 gives the keys to learning the skills presented. I present the skills in lesson form. Chapter 2 gives the features of each lesson. The largest chapter, Chapter 3, presents the lessons in order. Check the **Lessons Needed Before** feature as you progress.

This booklet contains lessons involving shooting technique, pivoting, and shooting practice. **The Basketball Player's Bible** contains the lessons presented here and many other related ones.

Golden Aura's Nitty-Gritty Basketball Series
by Sidney Goldstein

See the description in the back of this book.

The Basketball Coach's Bible

The Basketball Player's Bible

The Basketball Shooting Guide

The Basketball Scoring Guide

The Basketball Dribbling Guide

The Basketball Defense Guide

The Basketball Pass Cut Catch Guide

Basketball Fundamentals

Planning Basketball Practice

Videos for the Guides soon available

HOW TO CONTACT THE AUTHOR

The author seeks your comments about this book. Sidney Goldstein is available for consultation and clinics with coaches and players. Contact him at:

Golden Aura Publishing
PO Box 41012
Philadelphia, PA 19127
215 438-4459
current email (2/3/97): mrbball@idt.net
current web site: http://idt.net/~mrbball

Chapter One
1

Principles of Learning

How To Use The Shooting Guide

Start from the beginning and progress through the lessons one by one. Typically, I arrange them in order of increasing difficulty. You may want to skip some topics. However, use the **Lessons Needed Before** feature to insure that you do not omit needed techniques.

The most important as well as the most frequently skipped lessons involve techniques. If you spend the needed time on these lessons, you will improve exponentially on a daily basis. Skip them and improvement may be delayed for months and even years.

One big misconception about learning the basics is that to improve you must practice things millions of times. I've tried it and so has everybody else. It does not work well. Volume of practice does not necessarily bring about improvement; practicing properly insures improvement. The following **principles** tell you what and how to practice. A list of **Counterproductive Beliefs** follows. These often widely held ideas prevent learning because they do not work.

The Principles Of Shooting

1. Shooting improvement starts with technique. See lessons 1-4; Lesson 6 is for the layup.

2. Technique must be practiced close to the basket. See lessons 5, 7, and 8.

3. To improve your shooting range start close to the basket and gradually back off. See lessons 8 and 25.

4. To improve shooting you must shoot in a game-like situation. See lessons 9 and 26.

5. Every shooting move, as will as every other move to dribble or to pass, starts with a pivot. So, you must be an expert at pivoting. See lessons 10-12.

Counterproductive Beliefs

1. Repetition yields improvement. This is only true to a limited degree. Improvement only follows doing things correctly. Practicing incorrectly yields problems. If you practice correctly, follow the lessons, improvement will come with much less repetition than you initially thought.

2. Only 7th graders need to practice technique. Not true. Even Hall of Famers do. Every time you play ball you need to warm up with a few minutes of shooting technique.

3. Only 7th graders need to practice close to the basket. No, everybody does for several reasons. One is that this is the best way to use and apply technique. And again I say, without technique improvement, there is no improvement. The other reason is that a great percentage of shots are taken from this area in a game. So, it is most beneficial to practice game level shooting especially in this area.

4. You can work on technique as you work on shooting. Nope. Technique and shooting need to be practiced separately. One, technique improves your shot by changing and focusing on the mechanics (movement) of the shot. You give little thought to the actual shot when working on technique. Conversely or inversely or reciprocally, thinking about technique when in the motion of shooting can only psyche you out. These two things should be practiced, and even more importantly, thought about separately.

5. If you are a good shooter in practice, then you should be a good game shooter. No. Shooting rested, under little psychological pressure or physical defensive pressure in practice is not the same as shooting under more adverse game situations. Good shooters are good game shooters.

6. You need talent to shoot well. Only naturally talented players can shoot well and learn tricky moves. Not so. Anybody can be a good shooter or dribbler, passer, etc., if they practice properly.

7. Great shooters are great players. Not so. Note that many Hall of Famers are not great shooters. Shooting is only one part of the game. If you want to be a great basketball player, you need to be as tall, strong, quick, and fast as possible. Work on being an athlete as well as practicing the skills. All Hall of Famers are great athletes.

Chapter Two
2

Lesson Features

Table Information

At a glance this table gives an overview to aid in planning. It supplies the name and number of each lesson as well as these additional features: lessons needed before, the number of players needed, the effort level, the estimated practice times, whether you need a ball and/or a court. Practice the *no ball* or *no court* lessons for homework while watching TV or sitting down. The Player's Corner section of each lesson supplies some of the same information.

Number

The lessons are numbered in order from easiest to hardest, from most fundamental to most complicated. Typically, do them in order. Sometimes you can skip. If you do, check the **Lessons Needed Before** feature so that you do not skip essential lessons.

Name

A name related to each lesson serves as a descriptive mnemonic device (I almost forgot that). When skills are executed simultaneously, their names are directly coupled like Pivot Around Shoot or Jump Hook. Lessons with skills separately performed are named, for example, Pivot with Defense, where one player pivots on offense while the other is on defense.

Brief

In one sentence (usually) the **brief** immediately familiarizes you with the lesson by stating the action and movement involved.

Why Do This

When do you use this in a game? What is the significance of the lesson? What fundamentals do you practice? How does this lesson relate to others? The **Why Do This** section answers these questions.

Directions

These are step-by-step directions for you.

Key Points

This feature emphasizes important points in the directions so that you will not make common mistakes.

When You Are More Expert

These more expert lessons usually add another step, combine another skill, or change one variable in the previous lesson. Some lessons have as many as four expert additions.

Player's Corner and Section Tables

At a glance you can see that the **Player's Corner** lists 8 useful pieces of information about each lesson. The **Table of Lessons** in **Appendix C** and each **Section Table** contain this same information. **Xs** in the tables mean <u>yes</u>. Dashes (-) mean <u>no</u>.

• Lessons Needed Before

Do these lessons before this current one. If you don't, then you will have a problem. Often you can skip lessons without it being disastrous. Not so with the lessons listed as Lessons Needed Before.

• Additional Needs

This feature gives 4 useful pieces of information.

Ball and Court

For most lessons you need a **ball** and a **court**. However, for some either one or the other or both are not needed. These lessons can be practiced at home while watching TV or in your backyard. **Xs** in the tables mean <u>yes</u>.

Players

Most lessons are for individuals. So, the Player's Corner lists additional players needed, whereas the Tables give the total number (which is always one more than additional players).

Assist

For some lessons you need an inactive **assistant** to either act as a dummy player or more importantly to closely watch what you are doing. **Xs** in the tables mean <u>yes</u>.

• Effort or Effort Level

The effort level of a lesson involves the physical effort involved. Level 1 lessons involve technique. Do them slowly;

they often do not resemble the skill performed in a game because 2 to 5 technique lessons often comprise a skill. In situations calling for defense, the defense expends little effort.

Level 2 lessons are at the practice level. Any skill practiced at a moderate pace like shooting or pivoting is at level 2. This level is a catchall for lessons between levels 1 and 3. Defense against offense makes a moderate effort.

Level 3 lessons are at the game level. Players sprint and perform at maximum effort. Pressure is on players. Offense and defense go full speed against each other. Games are easy compared to these lessons.

• Daily Practice Time

This is a time range needed to practice this lesson. Note that many lessons have additional parts. These will take more time.

• More Expert Lessons

Each of these additions adds one or two parameters to the main lesson. Few are optional. Most need to be done after you are more expert.

FEATURES OF THE DIAGRAMS

Lines and Arrows

Solid lines indicate movement of players whereas dashed lines usually indicate movement of the ball. One exception is dashed lines used to show pivoting direction. The types of arrows used are solid for movement and hollow for passes. A different type of arrow head is used for fakes. See the diagrams.

Body Position of Player

The body of a player is shown from an overhead view two ways. The line or the ellipse represents the shoulders. The

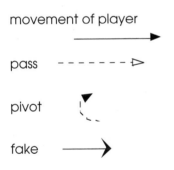

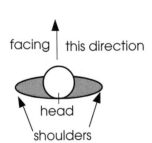

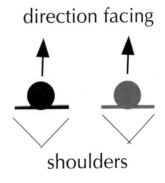

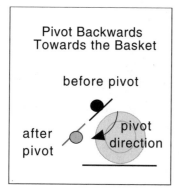

Pivot Backwards
Towards the Basket

before pivot

after pivot

pivot direction

circle shows the head. The player is always facing away from the shoulders toward the head.

Shades for Different Positions

When a player is shown in two positions in the same diagram, the first position is black and the second is lighter in color. Often offense or defense are shown in light and dark shades. In some diagrams shades are used to designate the position of a player when the ball of the same shade is in the diagramed position.

Numbers in Multistep Movements

Many drills involve multiple steps. Each step, as well, may have several timed movements that need to be executed in order. So, in the diagrams for each step, the numbers indicate the order of the movements. One (1) means first, two (2) second and so on. If two players move at the same time the numbers will be the same, so there may be several ones or twos in the diagram.

In the diagram below, there are three ones in the diagram. This indicates that these players move at the same time. There are two twos; one indicates a cut, while the other indicates a pass.

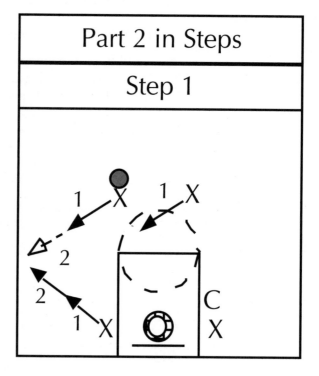

Part 2 in Steps

Step 1

Chapter Three

3

Shooting Technique Lessons 1-15

L E S S O N	NAME	A S S I S T	P L A Y E R S	C O U R T	B A L L	E F F O R T	L E S S O N	Lessons Before	REF TO *Coach's Manual*	DAILY TIME	E X T R A
1-15	**SHOOTING TECHNIQUE**										
1	The Magic Touch	-	1	-	x	1	1	none	1.0	1-2	0
2	Flick Your Wrist	x	1	-	-	1	2	none	3.0	2	0
3	Flick Up	x	1	-	x	1	3	2	5.1	2-5	2
4	One-Inch Shot	x	1	x	x	1	4	3	5.2	5-10	1
5	One-Foot Shot	x	1	x	x	2	5	4	5.3	5-15	2
N 6	The No-Step Layup 1-3	x	1	x	x	1	6	1	5.4	5-20	0
N 7	One Step & Dribble Layup 1-3	x	1	x	x	2	7	2	5.5	5-15	1
8	Foul Shot Technique 1-3	x	1	-	x	1	8	5	5.6	2-5	2
9	Foul Shot Practice	-	1	x	x	3	9	8	5.7	5-15	0
N 10	Start Pivoting	x	1	-	-	1	10	none	2.0	5-10	0
N 11	Pivoting with Ball	x	1	-	x	2	11	10	2.1	2-20	0
12	Pivot with Defense	-	2	-	x	2-3	12	11	2.2	5-10	3
13	Driving to the Basket	-	1	x	x	2	13	7	8.1	5-20	2
14	Near to Far	-	1	x	x	2	14	8	8.3	5-10	0
15	Full Court Shoot	-	1	x	x	2-3	15	13,14	8.2	5-20	1

N – Primarily for Novices
All other lessons are appropriate for players at all levels.

1 The Magic Touch

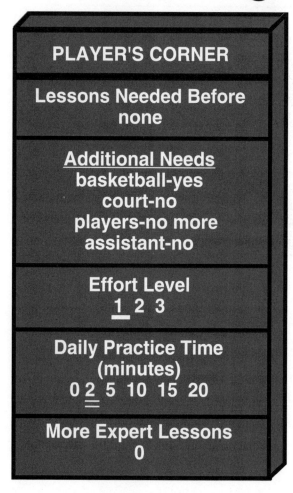

PLAYER'S CORNER

Lessons Needed Before
none

Additional Needs
basketball-yes
court-no
players-no more
assistant-no

Effort Level
<u>1</u> 2 3

Daily Practice Time (minutes)
0 <u>2</u> 5 10 15 20

More Expert Lessons
0

Brief:
Hold the ball in an exaggerated position.

Why Do This

The fingertips control the ball when you shoot, dribble, pass, and catch. This lesson overdoes the way to hold the ball. It improves your ability to shoot, pass, catch, and dribble without even practicing these skills. You can do this at any time during practice or at home. In the past you may have heard of a player who slept with a ball. Sounds funny, but some of the greats did it. It sensitized their fingertips, which enabled them to control the ball better. They awakened better players or at least better ball handlers!

Sensitivity is another name for *touch*, a word usually used in connection with shooting. However, *touch* is needed just as much for passing, catching, and dribbling. So, this lesson is important for learning all the ball handling skills, not just shooting.

Directions

1. Shape each hand into a claw and growl (like a *small* lion).

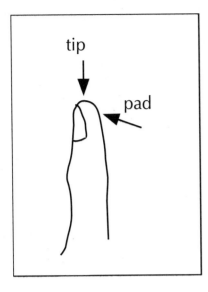

2. Hold the ball so that only the fingertips and finger ends touch the ball. Long fingernails make this difficult. They need to be cut.

3. Squeeze the ball tightly while you read about the importance of this.

Key Points

1. Claw your hands and growl (really).

2. Overdo it. Keep your palms far from the ball.

3. Spread your fingers as far apart as possible.

How to Practice

Do this for a minute every time you pick up the basketball. Do this while you are talking or listening at practice. You will never outgrow this lesson. If you are just starting to learn basketball, do this while you are watching TV. Use a volleyball, beach ball, or balloon if a basketball is not available.

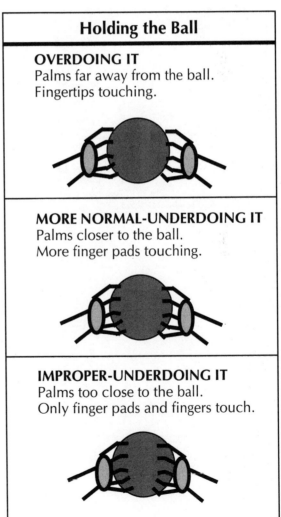

Holding the Ball

OVERDOING IT
Palms far away from the ball.
Fingertips touching.

MORE NORMAL-UNDERDOING IT
Palms closer to the ball.
More finger pads touching.

IMPROPER-UNDERDOING IT
Palms too close to the ball.
Only finger pads and fingers touch.

2 Flick Your Wrist

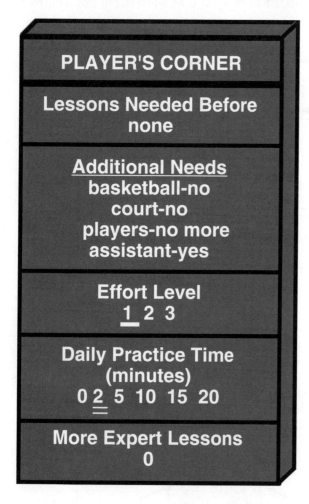

PLAYER'S CORNER

Lessons Needed Before
none

Additional Needs
basketball-no
court-no
players-no more
assistant-yes

Effort Level
<u>1</u> 2 3

Daily Practice Time
(minutes)
0 <u>2</u> 5 10 15 20

More Expert Lessons
0

Brief:
Move your wrist back and forth with the arms extended overhead.

Why Do This

This lesson is the key to learning all the ball handling skills - shooting, passing, and dribbling. Practice with the wrists significantly improves your shooting, passing, and dribbling without even touching a ball! Only a small amount of time is spent on this lesson, but the rewards are great. The consequences of skipping it, because you consider it too easy, are much greater. Count the good dribblers (or shooters or passers) on the court in any game from sixth grade level to a professional all-star game. It will not add up to ten, as it should. Some Hall of Famers do not even have the skills of many 12-year-olds. Professionals, and the rest of us as well, lack many fundamental skills because coaches usually work at more advanced levels. So, do it.

Directions

1. Let your arms hang loosely at your sides. To loosen your hands, shake them both back and forth and to the sides. The fingers and arms move like wet noodles. Continue for 10-30 seconds.

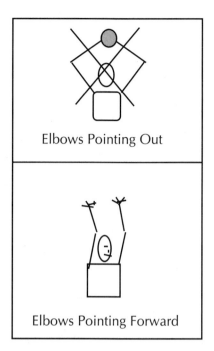

Elbows Pointing Out

Elbows Pointing Forward

2. Let your hands hang loosely at your sides again. Turn your arm so that the back of your hand is facing forward; the palms face backward. Let your arms and hands hang loosely. Using your arms, not the wrist or hand, flick your wrists forward only. Let them come back to the original position without using extra effort. The wrists and hands move like a waving wet noodle. The elbows are only slightly bent.

3. This type of wrist motion is used while dribbling. Do this for a minute on your own everyday. Your dribbling and as well as your shooting will improve.

4. Raise your arms directly overhead (like when the sheriff in a Western says, "Hands up") to practice the wrist movement in a shooting and passing position. Now the backs of the hands face backward; the palms face forward. The elbows are slightly bent forward, not to the sides. Rotate the elbows slightly inward to make the elbows point forward.

5. Loosen the wrists and hands. Flick your wrist and hand backward only. Let them come forward without additional effort. Continue this for 1-2 minutes.

Flicking Wrist

blow up of hand movement to right

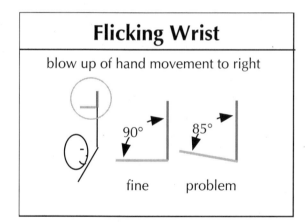

90°   85°

fine   problem

Key Points

1. This lesson is a key to learning how to shoot, dribble, and pass.

2. The hands and wrists need to be loose. The fingers are spread apart and loose.

3. The motion of the hand is forward and back, not sideways.

4. The elbows point slightly forward or back, not to the side.

5. Flick in one direction only, toward the back of the hand.

6. You will probably tire quickly. It may take several days to several weeks to feel comfortable doing this.

7. You must flick your wrist 90° back to shoot properly. Flicking even 5° less will prevent you from shooting well. Wrist problems also hamper passing and dribbling.

How to Practice

Practice this lesson every day of the season. Do it for 10-20 seconds before any type of shooting, passing, or dribbling practice. You will immediately see the benefits.

3 Flick Up

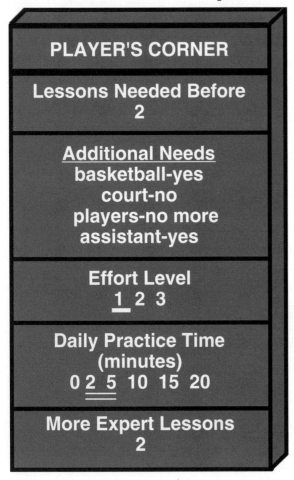

PLAYER'S CORNER

Lessons Needed Before
2

Additional Needs
basketball-yes
court-no
players-no more
assistant-yes

Effort Level
1 2 3

Daily Practice Time
(minutes)
0 2 5 10 15 20

More Expert Lessons
2

Use these cues for each step:

1. arms– arms overhead
2. elbow– move the elbow to-wards the nose
3. wrist– wrist back and twist forearm so that the wrist and hand face foreward
4. growl– claw the hand, ball on fingertips
5. flick

Brief:
Flick the ball up 1-2 feet and catch it on your fingertips.

Why Do This

This is another significant shooting lesson because your entire body is involved. I want you to use the right body parts to shoot the ball. Believe it or not–you do not shoot the ball with your arms. Many pros go into shooting slumps because they try to arm the ball up instead of shooting it properly. Use your legs and wrists to shoot. Besides developing touch, this lesson teaches you to use wrists and legs, not the arms.

Directions

1. The feet are shoulder width apart; both arms are extended straight overhead at shoulder width; the elbows are straight and pointing forward; the palms face forward.

2. Bend the wrist of your shooting hand back-ward as far as possible (do it with the other hand as well); claw the hand; balance the ball on the fingertips of the shooting hand first.

3. Move the elbow 2-3 inches inward toward your nose. Slightly rotate the forearm to the outside if necessary in order to keep the palm facing straight forward, not to the side. The shoulders and body remain facing forward. If you feel like you are in a straight jacket or that I am asking you to be a circus contortionist, you really need this lesson. It may take a week or so to feel comfortable doing this.

4. Flick the wrist so that the ball goes about one foot straight up. Do not use your legs or your arms, just your wrists.

5. Catch the ball on the fingertips of one hand and continue flicking it straight up for 1-3 minutes.

6. Switch hands. Flick and catch with the other hand for 1-3 minutes.

More Expert Lessons
Flick Up High

7. Repeat this lesson using the legs as well as the wrists to flick ball. Bend the legs, not the arms, and flick the ball with the wrist 3-6 feet high. Catch the ball with two hands. You need not do this with your opposite hand.

Shoot Up

8. Shoot the ball your normal way straight up 5-15 feet. Use your legs to get height, not your arms. Do not force the shot. Catch it with two hands. These are called shoot ups.

Key Points

1. It is beneficial to have someone watch you do this lesson.

2. The arms are overhead with only the slightest bend of the elbows; the feet are parallel to each other; the shoulders face straight forward, not toward the side. This is a common difficulty.

3. The hands are claw shaped; the wrist is bent back all the way; the wrist is flicked upward; the arms do not move. Do not use the legs until step 7 above.

4. If you have difficulty bending back the wrist, practice lesson 2. The more the wrist is bent the stronger the flick. As a result you need less arm movement to shoot the ball.

5. Your body needs to be aligned properly–head, shoulders, feet, arms, elbows face the shooting direction.

6. Do not use lots of effort to force the shoot up to hit the ceiling. The motion must be easy and natural, not forced.

How to Practice

Make sure you are expert both flicking and catching before you advance to the next step. If you feel contorted when you need to point your elbows forward, then you are not yet expert enough to continue. It may take weeks of practice before you are ready to advance. The most you can practice this is 5-10 minutes at any one time. You can practice this at home since you do not need a court. Again, use any other large ball if a basketball is not available.

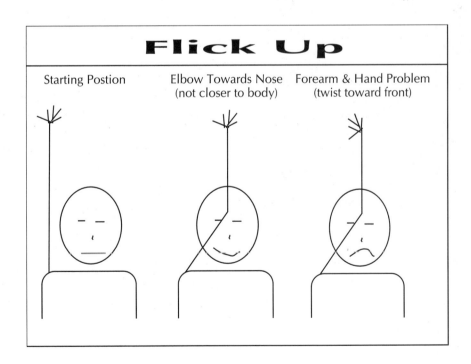

Flick Up

| Starting Postion | Elbow Towards Nose (not closer to body) | Forearm & Hand Problem (twist toward front) |

4 One-Inch Shot

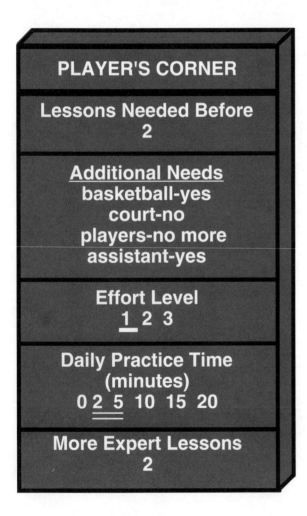

PLAYER'S CORNER

Lessons Needed Before
2

Additional Needs
basketball-yes
court-no
players-no more
assistant-yes

Effort Level
<u>1</u> 2 3

Daily Practice Time
(minutes)
0 <u>2</u> <u>5</u> 10 15 20

More Expert Lessons
2

Brief:
Shoot the ball from directly under the basket.

Why Do This

This technique level lesson forces you to extend your body, arms, and the ball to the maximum because the basket is directly overhead. It is difficult to shoot the ball improperly, even though some players succeed. Don't step away from the basket. Squaring up to the basket is introduced.

Directions

1. Start with your nose directly under the rim of the basket in the center position (middle of the lane). Mark the position with masking tape or another object so you do not step back.

2. You need to square up to the basket in the direction that you are going to shoot. In this lesson you are not going to shoot off the backboard. So, square up to the rim.

3. Here is how to square up: Put your arms straight in front of you like a sleepwalker. Your fingers point in the direction that you are going to shoot. Make sure that your arms and shoulders are at right angles (or perpendicular) to each other.

Squaring Up – Right and Wrong

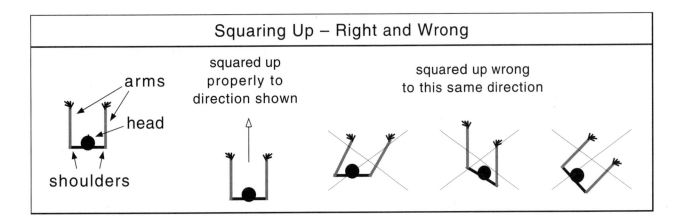

arms

head

shoulders

squared up
properly to
direction shown

squared up wrong
to this same direction

One-Inch Shot Setup

view from
above the basket

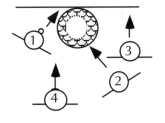 = player positions

---

Which players are squared up properly?

Write your answers here.

1 & 2 are squared up
  1 to the backboard
  2 to the rim

3 & 4 are not squared up

---

4. Shoot the ball without stepping backward. Use the wrist and the legs only. It will be difficult at first. Take your time.

5. The ball does not hit the ground at any time during this lesson. No dribbling. Get your own rebound. Shoot 10-20 shots.

More Expert Lessons

Change Position

6. Move to the right of the basket, then to the center, then to the left. Shoot over the rim; do not use the backboard.

Key Points

1. This is a shooting technique lesson. Do not take regular shots.

2. The ball does not hit the ground.

3. Square up in the direction that you shoot.

4. Even though this is an uncomfortable shooting position, too close to the basket, do not back off.

5. Players who benefit the most from this lesson have the greatest difficulty doing it initially.

6. Use cue words before shooting: Nose under rim, square up, hands overhead, wrist back, shoot.

How to Practice

Practice this lesson everyday until it becomes easy to do.

5 One-Foot Shot

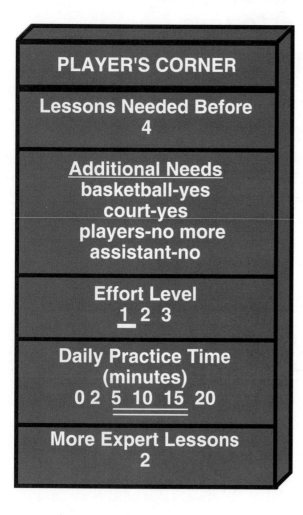

PLAYER'S CORNER

Lessons Needed Before
4

Additional Needs
basketball-yes
court-yes
players-no more
assistant-no

Effort Level
<u>1</u> 2 3

Daily Practice Time
(minutes)
0 2 <u>5 10 15</u> 20

More Expert Lessons
2

Brief:
Shoot one foot shots from the right, center, and left of the basket.

Why Do This
Step back one foot from the basket and shoot a near regular shot. This shot is between the technique and practice levels. However, practice technique before doing this. Here you will apply the technique that you have practiced in the previous lesson. I want to caution you about advancing to this lesson too quickly–it will be to your detriment. Without the proper technique you will be practicing an improper way to shoot. You will not improve. Stay with the technique as long as possible before going on. The only way to be a poor shooter is to practice improperly. Otherwise, there is no limit to how much you can improve. The proper way involves lots of technique practice and short shot practice.

Directions
1. Start one foot away from the basket on the right side of the basket. Shoot a nearly normal shot from one foot away from the basket.

One-Foot Shot Setup

Three Shooting Positions

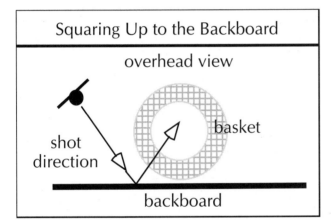

Squaring Up to the Backboard

overhead view

shot direction

basket

backboard

2. Use the backboard for each shot, even from the center position.

3. Pick a spot on the backboard to aim at; square up to this spot, not the basket; move the ball high overhead, then shoot.

4. Do not let the ball touch the ground while doing this lesson because this wastes half your time. This means no dribbling. Rebound your shot before it hits the ground.

5. Shoot 5 shots from each position–right, center, left–then rotate back again to the right. Lefties can reverse this direction.

Key Points

1. Square up to the backboard, then use it for each shot.

2. Set up one foot from the basket, not two or three.

3. Advance to this lesson only after your technique is proper. Otherwise, this and the other lessons will be a waste of your time.

How to Practice

Repeat this for 5-15 minutes everyday.

More Expert Lessons

Regular One Foot Shot

Repeat Lesson 5 taking a regular one foot shot. Do not worry about technique now. The technique lessons improved it. You need to shoot without thinking about technique. So, forget about it now. If your technique is not proper, go back to the technique lesson. Don't make this a technique lesson.

One Foot Jump Shot

This is the same as lesson 5 except you take one foot jump shots. The directions for the jump shot are simple–jump before you shoot. Initially use little effort on the jump. It is also better if you shoot on the way up. Note that there are many ways to take a jump shot–fadeaways (jumping away from the basket), shooting at the peak of the jump, jump hooks, and so on.

6 The No-Step Layup 1-3

Brief:
Younger players learn the mechanics of the layup in two steps without dribbling or running.

Why Do This

You can more readily learn the layup shot when it is taught by itself. Too often young players require months or even years to correctly execute the layup off the proper foot. After 15 minutes of this exercise you will notice remarkable improvement; in one week you will be an expert. Rebounding your own shot makes it less likely you will make common errors like broad jumping and floating too far underneath the basket before shooting. In part one, the movement is practiced without shooting. In part two, a layup is shot at the basket.

Directions
Part 1- No Shot Layup

1. The ball starts at waist height, feet shoulder width apart. Righties place the left foot one step forward, lefties the right foot, not surers put the left foot forward. You are righties now.

2. Twist the ball so that the right hand is on top. Left hand for lefties.

3. Put your weight on and step on the forward foot. Simultaneously move the ball up and the back leg forward and up. Do not bring the back foot down.

4. Your arms end up fully extended and the back leg is forward; the thigh is horizontal, the foot is off the floor.

5. Repeat this 10 to 50 times without shooting.

Part 2- Shoot the Layup

(See the diagram showing starting spots on the left, right and center.)

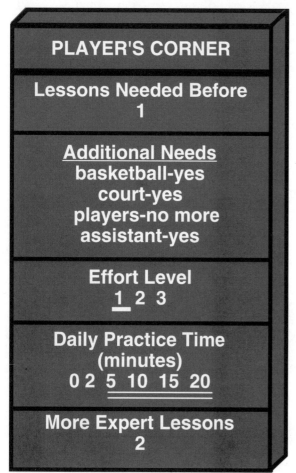

PLAYER'S CORNER

Lessons Needed Before
1

Additional Needs
basketball-yes
court-yes
players-no more
assistant-yes

Effort Level
<u>1</u> 2 3

Daily Practice Time (minutes)
0 2 <u>5 10 15 20</u>

More Expert Lessons
2

Layup Steps

Step 1   Step 2   Steps 3-4

Layup Shooting Positions

6. To shoot the layup, start 2 feet from the basket on the right side. Lefties start on the left side. Do not start far away from the basket because you are taking a small step.

7. Use the painted rectangle or any other blemish on the backboard as a place to aim. Square up to the spot where you aim.

8. The cues for the layup are: foot forward, turn ball, move ball up and back leg forward, shoot.

9. Shoot, get your own rebound, then without dribbling, return to the same spot. The ball does not touch the floor.

10. Repeat this 10-20 times.

Part 3- Switch Sides

11. Switch sides. Righties shoot a left side layup the same way as you did on the right side. Lefties do not change the movements on the right side. Do 10-20 layups.

12. Move to the center 2 feet from the basket. The center layup is the most difficult. Use the backboard in the center as well. Repeat 10-20 times.

Key Points

1. Find an assistant to work with you on this.

2. Square up to a chosen spot on the backboard.

3. Start with one step forward.

4. Be expert in steps 1-5 before doing the layup with shooting.

How to Practice

If you have difficulty doing the layup, practice without shooting to get the hang of it. Get someone to work with you. Stay on this for several days if necessary.

7 One Step & Dribble Layup 1-3

PLAYER'S CORNER

Lessons Needed Before
6

Additional Needs
basketball-yes
court-yes
players-no more
assistant-yes

Effort Level
1 <u>2</u> 3

**Daily Practice Time
(minutes)**
0 2 <u>5</u> <u>10</u> <u>15</u> 20

More Expert Lessons
3

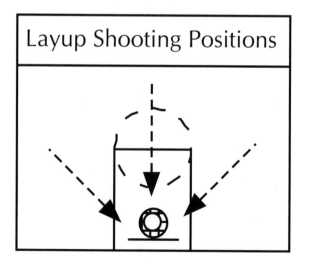

Layup Shooting Positions

Brief:
Take one step and a dribble before shooting the layup.

Why Do This
If you are running down court to shoot a layup in a game, the most important step is the last one. In this lesson this last step is practiced. This lesson also combines the layup with dribbling. After a dribble step, a one step layup is taken. This last step (and a half—the half occurs when you bring up the back foot when shooting) before shooting is a slow step or a step used to slow down.

Directions
Part 1- One Step Layup
1. Start at a mark on the floor about 2-4 feet from the basket. If you can't find one in the right place, use a piece of masking tape to mark the spot. Righties start on the right; lefties on the left.

2. Take a step with the left foot (right foot for lefties) and then shoot the layup. Use the backboard. Gradually increase this step from a short one to a long one.

3. Go straight up rather than float forward under the basket. Floating makes the shot more difficult. It also puts you in a bad position, under the backboard, to rebound.

4. Then get your own rebound without letting the ball hit the floor.

5. Repeat this 5-15 times form the right, then center, and then the left.

Part 2- Step and Dribble
6. Take a dribble along with this first step. Start from a half down position so the dribble is low. Half down means that the knees, not the back, are bent. If you need to look down at the

ball don't dribble. Do some of the dribbling lessons before continuing.

7. Repeat this 10 times at each position–right, center, and left of the basket.

Part 3- Two Steps and a Dribble

8. Set up to do a one dribble layup and then take one step backward away from the basket. Now you are going to take a two step layup with one dribble.

9. Take one short step with the right foot (left for lefties) and then one longer one with the left. Dribble as you take the first step. Repeat 10 times from each position.

More Expert Lessons

Moving Back

10. Move another step back and take another dribble. Righties footwork is left, right, left; lefties–right, left, right.

11 Take 2 dribbles; one on the first step and one on the second.

12. Repeat this layup 10 times from each position.

Key Points

1. Stay in a half down position when dribbling.

2. On the last step go straight up, not forward, so you do not float under the basket.

3. This last step is more important than the ones before, so spend most of your time working on a one step layup without dribbling.

4. As your expertise increases, take longer last steps.

How to Practice

Spend most of your time on the one step layup without dribbling. If you have not completed dribbling lessons, then skip all the dribbling. Dribbling improperly makes you an expert at dribbling improperly. You don't want this to happen.

8 Foul Shot Technique 1-3

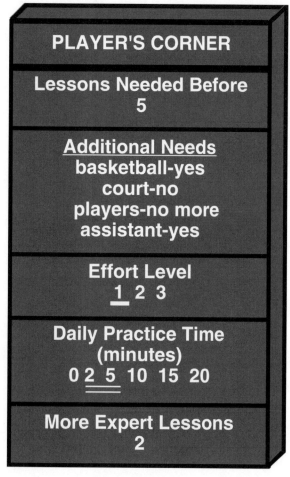

PLAYER'S CORNER

Lessons Needed Before
5

Additional Needs
basketball-yes
court-no
players-no more
assistant-yes

Effort Level
<u>1</u> 2 3

Daily Practice Time (minutes)
0 <u>2</u> <u>5</u> 10 15 20

More Expert Lessons
2

Foul Shot Setup

Brief:
Preliminary steps and tips for shooting foul shots in a game are given.

Why Do This

Foul shots are always done under great pressure in a game. Often the score is close. Invariably the game is momentarily stopped so that every person in the gym focuses on the shooter. This lesson helps you relax and concentrate on the mechanics of the shot.

At every level, junior high to professional, players regularly miss foul shots in game deciding situations. The techniques presented here remedy most of the causes. One special cause is that players do not shoot at their normal speed. Being more cautious, they slow down the movements of the arms, legs, and wrists to prevent mistakes. This becomes the mistake; you must shoot at a normal speed. Another reason why players miss foul shots at the end of the game is that they are a little tired, and their muscles, especially the leg muscles, are stiff. As a result they arm the ball up to the basket instead of shooting with the wrists and legs. This lesson shows you how to correct and prevent these problems.

Directions
Part 1- Shoot Up

1. Start with the ball on the ground. The feet are shoulder width apart.

2. Shake the wrists to loosen them.

3. Dribble the ball a few times with two hands. In the game you have very little chance to touch the ball. Handling it helps your touch and wrist movement.

4. Shoot the ball straight up a few feet at the **normal speed**, not at a slowed down pace which throws the normal shot off. I have seen numerous players in win-lose situations be too careful. Slowing down their shooting time causes problems. Often I have seen entire teams do this and shoot horrendously. Slow down before the shot, then shoot at normal speed.

5. Bend the knees a few times to the half down position–halfway between standing up and squatting. This helps you loosen up and reminds you to bend the legs when shooting.

6. Take a deep breath or two. This helps to calm you down. Hold your breath while you take the shot, just like a gun shooter does. This steadies your movement.

7. Repeat this procedure 3 or more times. Use cue words– Wrists, Ball, Knees, Breath.

Part 2- Half Distance Shot + Sprint

A foul shot is such a long shot that it often causes your shooting technique to fall apart. This lesson uses a shorter shot with the expectation that the longer shot will develop. Remember that practicing from the foul line before you are ready makes you an expert at doing it improperly. Wait till your shooting technique improves.

Shooting fully rested in practice is also a waste of time. In a game players shoot two fouls at a time while sweating. This lesson emulates this. Do this lesson last in any practice session to insure that you are tired.

8. Set up three feet from the basket on the line marking the boundary of the jump circle. If the gym is crowded it's okay to set up slightly to the right or left of the center.

9. Use the foul shooting technique cues: wrists, ball, knees, breath.

10. After shooting 2 shots, sprint, dribbling the ball, to the other end of the court (or anywhere) before shooting again. You need to sweat and be out of breath like you are in a game.

11. Repeat this as many times as possible within a 5-15 minute practice period.

Part 3- Move Back to Foul Line

12. Repeat steps 8-11 stepping closer to the foul line, away from the basket, after each sprint. Do not move past your normal shooting range. You are past your range if you need to use more effort to reach the basket.

Key Points

1. Use these cues before each shot:

• Wrists–shake them.

- Ball–handle it. Dribble and shoot up.
- Knees–bend halfway down.
- Breath–take a deep breath (or two) before the shot.

2. Do not slow down your shot movements.

3. Shoot at short distances from the basket until your technique develops.

4. As your technique develops, move one step at a time toward the foul line, away from the basket.

5. When your technique develops, sprint after every two shots to get out of breath like you are in a game.

How to Practice

Always practice technique before doing any shooting lesson. Practice 5-15 minutes when you are tired, not fresh. You may spend most or even all of the season (and the next) at the 3 foot distance. It's okay. Don't force a shot from the foul line. This causes more problems. It won't help your shooting either.

9 Foul Shot Practice

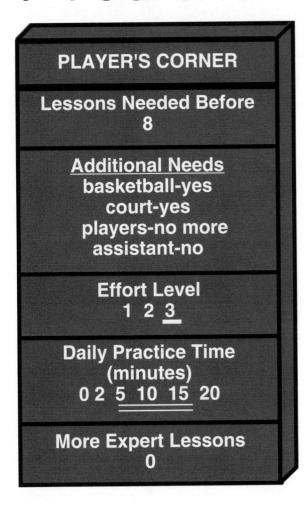

PLAYER'S CORNER

Lessons Needed Before
8

Additional Needs
basketball-yes
court-yes
players-no more
assistant-no

Effort Level
1 2 **3**

Daily Practice Time
(minutes)
0 2 **5 10 15** 20

More Expert Lessons
0

Foul Shot Setup

Possible positions

Brief:
This lesson gives players game-like foul shooting practice.

Why Do This

This is the most difficult shooting lesson in the book. A big mistake is to do it prematurely. Wait till you have both the shooting and foul shooting techniques down pat at shorter distances.

Foul shooting practice often involves shooting 10, or even 20, shots in a row. Here are several reasons why this is not effective:

1. You need to work on shooting technique, rather than shooting.

2. You need to shoot closer to the basket and then gradually move to the foul line.

3. In a game you are more tired, out of breath, and under greater pressure than when shooting fouls at practice.

To overcome these pitfalls, practice foul shooting addresses shooting technique as well as the game situation. It is best done when you are tired.

Directions

1. Shoot twice at one basket and then sprint down court to the other basket. Sprint back and forth several times if necessary.

2. Shoot before you catch your breath. Shoot from any position available on the foul line if other players are nearby. Move to one side if necessary. Don't wait for a center position.

3. Use the foul shooting technique cues–wrists, ball, knees, breath.

•The details arc in lesson 8.

4. Repeat.

Key Points

1. This is the most difficult shooting lesson in the book. It is only effective if your technique is proper. Otherwise, practicing this will be counterproductive.

2. Shoot before you catch your breath.

How to Practice

Practice this every day when you are ready.

10 Start Pivoting

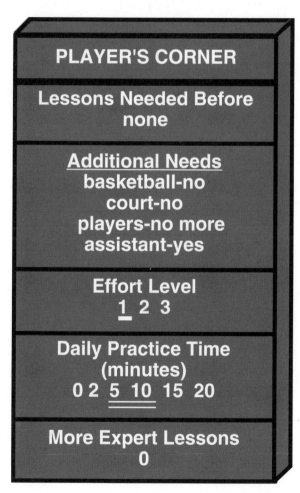

PLAYER'S CORNER

Lessons Needed Before
none

Additional Needs
basketball-no
court-no
players-no more
assistant-yes

Effort Level
<u>1</u> 2 3

Daily Practice Time
(minutes)
0 2 <u>5</u> <u>10</u> 15 20

More Expert Lessons
0

Brief:
Players pivot forward and backward with each foot.

Why Do This

You must pivot every time you touch the ball. Your ability to shoot, pass, catch, and rebound depends on your ability to pivot. So, you need to be expert in pivoting before you can perfect these other skills.

Directions

1. The feet are shoulder width apart.

2. Start with the left foot as the pivot foot. Put all of your weight on the ball of the left foot. Then shift your weight to the right foot.

3. Do these actions together. Move the right foot forward, making a circle around the left foot, swiveling (pivoting) on the ball of the left foot. Act like you are stomping on bugs with the right foot.

Make 2-4 revolutions. An assistant should watch the ball of the foot for sliding.

4. Now, stomp on bugs moving backward. Make 2-4 revolutions.

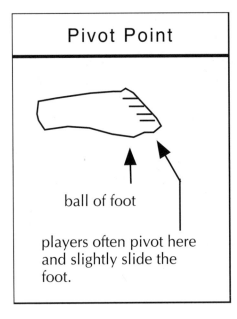

Pivot Point

ball of foot

players often pivot here and slightly slide the foot.

5. Now, switch the pivot foot. Put all of your weight on the ball of the right foot. Switch your weight to the left foot.

6. Repeat the directions to pivot forward and then backward.

Key Points

1. Stomping on bugs works better than more technical descriptions.

2. Pivot slowly, unless you want to be dizzy. Initially, small steps are better than large ones.

3. Assistants watch closely to make sure that: 1) players pivot on the ball of foot and 2) that players do not slide the foot while pivoting.

4. Players tend to pivot on some part of the foot other than the ball, such as the toes. Note that you can, by the rules, pivot on any part of the body without walking. These parts include the toes, behind, or even the head. This is more a factor when players scramble on the floor for the ball. However, using the ball of the foot is the most practical and easiest way to pivot.

5. Watch for sliding of the ball of the foot. This is a walking violation.

How to Practice

Repeat this lesson during warm-ups or after warm downs or for homework. A homework assignment can be 100 pivots, twenty-five each way: forward and back on the left foot; repeat with the right foot.

Practicing this for two weeks, everyday, is sufficient for anybody. As soon as possible, advance to the next lesson that involves pivoting with the ball. More experienced players can start there.

11 Pivoting with Ball

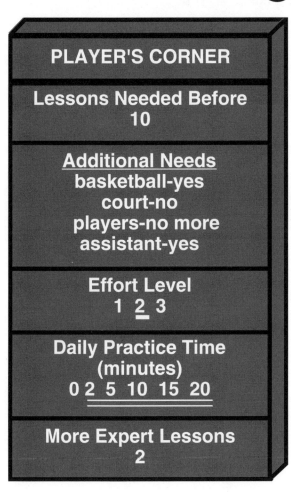

PLAYER'S CORNER

Lessons Needed Before
10

Additional Needs
basketball-yes
court-no
players-no more
assistant-yes

Effort Level
1 **2** 3

Daily Practice Time
(minutes)
0 **2** **5** **10** **15** **20**

More Expert Lessons
2

Brief:
Pivot while moving the ball high and low, left and right, and close and far from the body.

Why Do This
Pivoting, as previously discussed, is applicable to everything done with the basketball. This lesson combines pivoting with ball movement. You can use the ball movement to keep the ball away from opponents as well as fake before either shooting, passing, or dribbling. This skill is the key to all offensive moves.

Directions
1. Hold the ball at waist height, feet shoulder width apart. The left foot is the pivot foot.

2. Take one long step to the right and push the ball to the far right, low to the ground. The ball is to the right of your foot.

3. Pivot 180 degrees forward, halfway around, and simultaneously push the ball high overhead.

4. Repeat this twice forward and then twice pivoting backward.

5. Switch the pivot foot and repeat pivoting forward and back-ward.

6. Repeat the entire lesson several times. Take longer steps as you become more expert.

Key Points

1. Pushing the ball is a quick powerful movement.

2. Use these verbal cues as you do the lesson: stretch low, pivot high.

3. Initially concentrate on learning the routine. Gradually work to improve the movements.

How to Practice

Most lessons in this book involve pivoting. The applications are almost endless. Novices cannot practice this enough at the beginning of the season. Do it for homework or during any warm-up. All offensive moves start here. That is why this is such a pivotal lesson.

12 Pivot with D

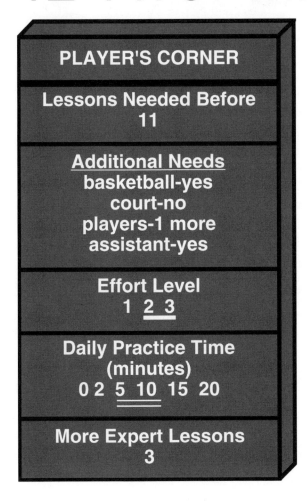

PLAYER'S CORNER

Lessons Needed Before
11

Additional Needs
basketball-yes
court-no
players-1 more
assistant-yes

Effort Level
1 <u>2</u> 3

Daily Practice Time (minutes)
0 2 <u>5 10</u> 15 20

More Expert Lessons
3

Brief:
The offense pivots away from a defensive player attempting to steal the ball.

Why Do This
You pivot here in a game-type situation. Move the ball away from the defense as well as look to pass under pressure. The defense goes after the ball without fouling.

Directions
1. The offensive player starts with the left foot as pivot foot, ball waist high. The defense is 2 feet away.

2. The directions for the defense are simple–go after the ball without fouling. Move around the offense for the ball. Don't stop moving. This is a hustle lesson for the defense.

3. The offense pivots backward and forward holding the ball in the high-low, left-right, close-far positions practiced in Lesson 11. Do not keep your back to the defense. Face up to the defense and move the ball and the body to prevent a steal or tie-up.

4. The defense, while moving slowly, counts to 5, then stops. The offense calls fouls.

5. Repeat with the offense pivoting on the right foot.

6. Then switch roles.

Key Points
1. The defense must go after the ball very aggressively; more so than even in a game. The offense gets better practice this way.

2. The offense does more than just pivot away from the defense. This would defeat the purpose of the lesson. The offense faces up to the defense, preventing a steal by moving the ball and the body.

3. Remind the defense that flailing their arms, even without any contact, usually results in a foul call.

4. Do not slide the pivot foot.

5. Repeat this lesson and the others using the left and then the right foot as pivot foot.

More Expert Lessons

Pivot with Pass

During the lesson the assistant asks the pivoter for a pass. This is a more realistic situation. Use only hand gestures to get the pivoter's attention, since the purpose is to make the pivoter look around while protecting the ball. Make it more difficult for the passer by constantly moving around and by asking for a pass after variable amounts of time; one second one time, 5 seconds another. Always ask immediately if the passer is not looking.

Pivot with 2 on D

Position another defensive player behind the pivoter. With two defenders the offense pivots to keep the back to one while moving the ball away from the other. In a sense, the offense must always keep one defender boxed out. The offensive player needs to push the ball hard, like in Lesson 11, low to the far left or right and then pivot 180 degrees.

Pivot Pass with 2 on D

Repeat the previous lesson with an assistant asking for a pass with hand gestures.

13 Driving to the Basket

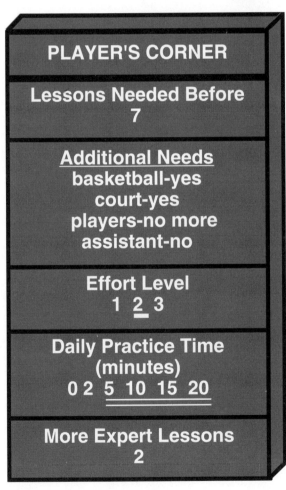

PLAYER'S CORNER

Lessons Needed Before
7

Additional Needs
basketball-yes
court-yes
players-no more
assistant-no

Effort Level
1 <u>2</u> 3

Daily Practice Time
(minutes)
0 2 <u>5</u> <u>10</u> <u>15</u> <u>20</u>

More Expert Lessons
2

Brief:
From the foul line you drive left and right starting with either foot as the pivot.

Why Do This
Players get their steps together for each drive like a hurdler getting steps together between hurdles. Righties always shoot off the left foot and lefties off the right foot. For moments when righties use the left hand they are considered lefties; lefties using the right hand are considered righties. Practice the four possible drives in this order (eight if you practice with both hands):

1. Left foot as pivot and go right.

2. Right foot as pivot and go right.

3. Left foot as pivot and go left.

4. Right foot as pivot and go left.

Do these at a moderate pace; no need to go quickly. Slow down if you encounter difficulty or feel awkward.

Directions
1. Start from a half down position with the ball at waist height.

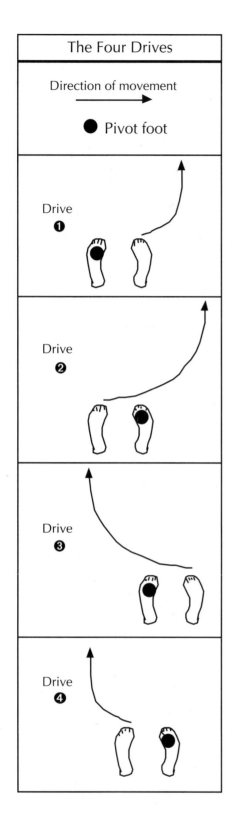

The Four Drives

Direction of movement →

● Pivot foot

Drive ❶

Drive ❷

Drive ❸

Drive ❹

2. Push the ball low, far to the side of the drive.

3. The first step is a long one, so that you get past the defense.

4. You must step around the defense, not through them, so move slightly sideways before moving forward. Use a chair or another person as dummy defense to step around.

5. Dribble the ball as you take the first step.

6. Do not drag the pivot foot.

7. Right handers always shoot off the left foot on either side of the basket and left handers always off the right foot.

8. Novice players take as many steps and dribbles as necessary to complete the move, whereas experienced, taller players can limit the steps to between 2 and 4.

9. Use only 1 or 2 dribbles. Do each drive 10 times if it feels uncomfortable, five otherwise.

10. Experienced players repeat this lesson with the opposite hand.

Key Points

1. Have someone watch you for dragging the pivot foot and stepping before dribbling..

2. Use a chair or another person as a defensive player to drive around. Step around the defense on the first step. When past the defense, reach around and out with the inside elbow to keep the defense behind.

3. Practice slowly. Speed naturally increases with repetition. You need to feel comfortable while practicing.

4. Always shoot off the left foot when shooting with the right hand and off the right foot when shooting with the left hand.

5. Push the ball far to the side of the drive low to the ground.

More Expert Lessons

Fake Then Drive

Players often fake before driving. Execute the fake slowly so the defense has time to react. The defense can't react to a quick fake. Two types of fakes are used. Do each drive 5-10 times.

1. A step fake is used before the crossover step in drive 2 and 3 above. (a. Right foot as pivot and go right. b. Left foot as pivot and go left.)

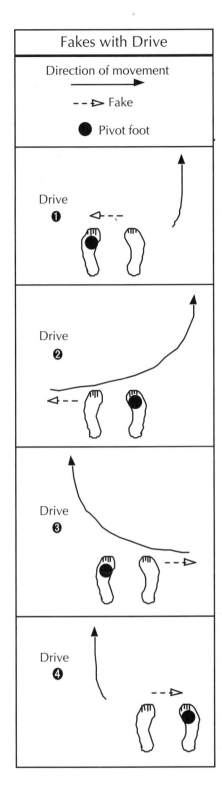

Fakes with Drive

Direction of movement →

- - ▷ Fake

● Pivot foot

Drive ❶

Drive ❷

Drive ❸

Drive ❹

2. Slowly push the ball and the body away from the pivot foot as you step in that same direction.

3. Bring the ball back, take the crossover step more quickly, and drive to the basket.

4. Do each drive 5 times.

5. Use a ball body fake for drives 1 and 4 above. (**a.** Left foot as pivot and go right. **b.** Right foot as pivot and go left.)

6. Push the ball and slightly turn the body in the opposite direction of the drive.

7. Then take a step and move the ball low to the outside direction of the drive.

Drive Opposite Foot

•This is only for experienced players for two reasons. One, this lesson undoes the fundamentals you are learning. Two, this move is only needed to beat very tall players.

•This layup is taken off the wrong foot on purpose. The advantage is that the defense is not ready for it. They expect you to take one and a half steps before shooting. This is especially effective against big players.

•Do this opposite foot drive using the same four moves as in the more regular drives. The layup is usually released one step farther from the basket than normal.

14 Near to Far

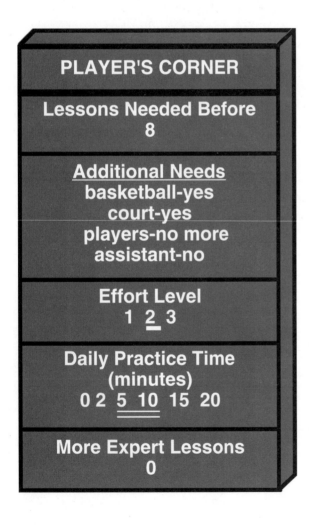

PLAYER'S CORNER

Lessons Needed Before
8

Additional Needs
basketball-yes
court-yes
players-no more
assistant-no

Effort Level
1 <u>2</u> 3

**Daily Practice Time
(minutes)**
0 2 <u>5 10</u> 15 20

More Expert Lessons
0

Brief:

You start close to the basket and step back one step after each made shot.

Why Do This

This is a great way for novices, in particular, to increase shooting range. Stepping back one foot at a time allows you to find your current range and then adjust to longer distances. Make adjustments for longer shots with the legs rather than the arms. This type of lesson is especially beneficial if you want to improve foul shooting or shooting from the corner.

Shooting involves more technique than most people realize. As you move farther from the basket, shooting technique can fall apart. If it does, practice shooting turns out to be practice shooting improperly. This lesson curbs this tendency.

A note of caution: this is a practice level lesson. Real shooting improvement only comes when you practice shooting in a game-like situation where you are running back and forth down the court with defense. So do not shoot too many, more than 5 or 10, shots from any one position.

If you are happy with your range, then shoot this same shot running full court solo, Lesson 15, or one-on-one.

Directions

1. Start close to the basket and take one step away only when you make a shot.

2. Keep moving back until you reach the distance you want.

3. If you miss two shots in a row, step forward towards the basket.

4. Use the backboard as much as possible when you are at an angle to the basket.

Key Points

1. Take a step back only when you make the shot.

2. Move toward the basket if you miss two in a row. If you miss two in a row, you are probably shooting too far from the basket or you need more practice at the technique level, Lessons 1-5.

3. Your shooting will improve if you practice close to the basket. If you exceed your range then your shooting may get worse or stay the same.

4. Warm up with the wrist flick and other technique lessons.

5. When you make 5 in a row, practice from another position or practice this shot running full court.

15 Full Court Shoot

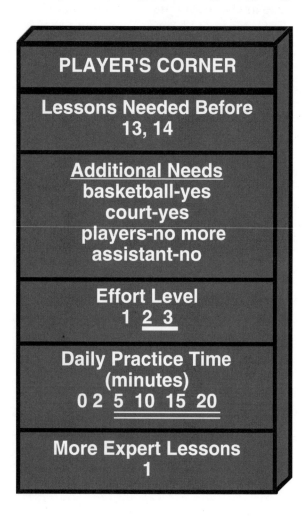

PLAYER'S CORNER

Lessons Needed Before
13, 14

Additional Needs
basketball-yes
court-yes
players-no more
assistant-no

Effort Level
1 2 3

Daily Practice Time
(minutes)
0 2 5 10 15 20

More Expert Lessons
1

Brief:

A player dribbles back and forth from one basket to another shooting at each basket.

Why Do This

In a game players shoot while out of breath after sprinting down court many times. Shots are not taken 10 in a row while you are nice, tidy, and rested. A good game shooter practices in a game-like way. This lesson gives you a way. You run full court shooting one shot at each basket. More time is spent dribbling in this lesson than shooting. So, switch hands on a regular basis. Try behind the back, between the legs dribbles often. It is a good idea to practice dribbling lessons before trying this one.

Directions

1. Run down one end and shoot. Get the rebound. Run down the other end and shoot. It is optional, though a good idea sometimes, to follow the shot up if you miss. Pace yourself.

2. Quickly go for the rebound. Make a quick transition.

3. Switch the dribbling hand regularly. Trick dribble between the legs and behind the back often. Keep the body and ball low, even though there is no defense.

4. Shoot from the distance that you need to practice. Keep shots short and move away from the basket one foot at a time. You can shoot one foot shots, layups, three foot shots off the backboard or even two foot corner shots. You can also practice foul shots and shots from three point range.

5. Run for 5-20 minutes.

Key Points

1. This is particularly helpful to experienced players practicing long shots. Novice players work on short shots.

2. Novice players, in particular, need to dribble with the head up and the ball low to the ground. Practice dribbling technique before doing this.

3. Warm up with other shooting lessons at the technique or practice levels before doing this. Work on the wrists, Lesson 2, and flick ups, Lesson 3, and other lessons like 4 and 5.

4. Don't do anything here that you can't do in a game. Don't stop or run patterns on the court that you would not do in a game. For example, bring the ball down court staying near the center rather than near the sideline. To take a corner shot veer off to one side or the other just before you reach the top of the key. Don't dribble to the foul line and then head for a three point shot in the corner.

More Expert Lessons

One-on-One Full Court

Play one-on-one full court to practice any shot or move. Don't necessarily play to win. Play to practice a move that you have been working on, whether it be an underneath hook or a 3 point corner shot. If the defense is tough, use this as an opportunity to practice against whatever the defense does best. If you know you can run in for layups against this opponent, try other moves. If the opponent is much taller, you may want to practice short jump shots or layups off the wrong foot. Again, use this for more than just a game to win; don't keep score; ask the other player if he or she wants extra effort on defense or whatever. After you shoot, quickly move to either rebound or make the transition back to defense.

What coaches say about *The Basketball Coach's Bible*

"I've never read anything more detailed regarding the fundamentals."

"I definitely would recommend this to ... anyone who wants to teach youngsters the finer points of the game."

Dale Brown, LSU Coach

"I can say, without question, that this is an excellent tool for teaching the fundamentals."

"The great game of basketball is broken down into simple terms. Congratulations on a job well done."

Jim Calhoun, UConn Coach

"This book is not only for the young coach, but it is also appropriate for coaches, experienced or not, at all levels."

"Young basketball players will be better trained, if coaches use your methods."

Charlene Curtis, former Temple U Coach

"It is one of the best teachers and guides for beginning coaches of young teams that I've seen."

Jack Mckinney, Former NBA Coach

"What a wonderful basic resource .... It gave me the perfect information to coach effectively and with confidence."

John Been, Prairie duSac, WI

"Your discussions of a planned agenda for every practice has inspired me for two years now and, in a great part, is responsible for my success during this time."

Tom Luker, 7th grade Coach

"Anyone interested in coaching basketball, from volunteer youth coach to high school coach, should read this book."

Jon Wilson, PA Director of Biddy Basketball

"[Y]our book was a huge help. I highly recommend this book to all coaches, young or experienced."

"By following the steps in your book I won the City Championship in my first year of coaching.

Scott Wiley, Harrison HS, Leesburg , IN

"[A] splendid job. I wish there was a similar book when I began coaching."

"Speedy" Morris, LaSalle University Coach

"People who know basketball, coaches who care about players, say this is the best book on fundamentals they have seen."

Robert Kuiserling, Odessa, MO, Youth Coach

"An outstanding learning tool for all ages. A must read for all coaches."

Stephanie Gaitley, St. Joseph's Univ. Coach

"The Basketball Coach's Bible is a great resource."

Phil Jackson, Chicago Bulls

"Great for any level of coaching. Being a fundamental fanatic, this is the best guide I have seen."

John Cornet, High School Coach, Tenafly, NJ

"Without question it is a very good book about fundamental basketball."

Tom Shirley, Phila. Textiles, AD & Coach

"The Basketball Bibles are the best books I have seen on the subject. Purchasing them is the best money I've spent."

Gregory S Bigg, Coach, Howell, NJ

"Thank you for your efforts in putting this book together. It has proved invaluable... throughout our 7-12 program."

Steve Hartman, Beatrice, Nebraska, Coach

"My girls really benefited from this great program of individual and group skill development."

Jennifer Lynch, Youth Coach, Edmond, OK

"The ideas in this book will be as helpful for you as they were for our team."

Bernie Ivens, former West Phila. HS Coach

"A coach's dream. A must for a beginning or experienced coach."

Lurline Jones, University City High School

The Coach's Bible is a real winner! It offers a thorough insight into the basic foundations of basketball. A truly outstanding book. If you love basketball, you will love **The Coach's Bibl**e."

Jim Tucker, Englewood High School Coach

"The practice tips are fantastic and (I) have really improved my shot..."

Nathan Miller, HS player, Bloomsberg , PA

"Your book is one on the best I've ever read."

Daniel Freeman III, Coach, Charlotte, NC

"Fantastic! A book like this is long overdue."

Bob Huggins, University of Cincinnati

"[T]he best book on teaching basketball. ...Your book has been so helpful... [W]e always tell Sister Jean and Father Brady, as Catholic coaches, [that] we read the Bible every night, ...[though] we never tell them which Bible we are reading."

Albert Balingit, Holy Spirit School, Sacramento, CA

APPLAUDED BY COACHES!

The NITTY-GRITTY BASKETBALL SERIES Is Here

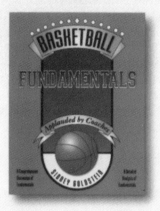

BASKETBALL FUNDAMENTALS
Applauded by Coaches
SIDNEY GOLDSTEIN

THE BASKETBALL COACH'S BIBLE
Applauded by Coaches
SIDNEY GOLDSTEIN
A Comprehensive and Systematic Guide to Coaching
A Detailed Explanation of Every Aspect of the Game

PLANNING BASKETBALL PRACTICE
Applauded by Coaches
SIDNEY GOLDSTEIN

THE BASKETBALL SHOOTING GUIDE
Applauded by Coaches
SIDNEY GOLDSTEIN

THE BASKETBALL PLAYER'S BIBLE
Applauded by Coaches
SIDNEY GOLDSTEIN

THE BASKETBALL SCORING GUIDE
Applauded by Coaches
SIDNEY GOLDSTEIN

THE BASKETBALL DRIBBLING GUIDE
Applauded by Coaches
SIDNEY GOLDSTEIN

THE BASKETBALL PASS CUT CATCH GUIDE
Applauded by Coaches
SIDNEY GOLDSTEIN

THE BASKETBALL DEFENSE GUIDE
Applauded by Coaches
SIDNEY GOLDSTEIN

we've got
books, videos
and clinics too
Nitty-Gritty Basketball Order Form

Visit our website for current pricing & availability
mrbasketball.net

Videos

Home use $32.95, Organization library use $39.95 Check for current prices and discounts. Videos follow books.

1. Fundamentals I (77-6) Covers all individual skills in order in the bible. Over 100 drills. 48 min

2. Fundamentals II (90-3) Covers all team skills in the bible in order including plays. 42 min

3. Planning Practice I (75-X) Goes through practice showing all drills including those not in other videos. 41 min

4. Planning Practice II (76-8) Forty ways to get more out of practice and each player. 41 min

5. Shooting I (78-4) Techniques that yield rapid and permanent improvement. 35 minutes

6. Shooting II (79-2) The basic shots as well as moves +sensible ways to practice. 47 minutes

7. Shooting III (80-6) Players shoot as well in a game as they do in practice. Foul shooting and shooting under pressure. 43 minutes

8. Dribbling (81-4) Anyone can be a good dribbler. These methods show how. 36 minutes

9. Defense I (84-9) On-ball defense including forcing and covering shooter. 39 minutes

10. Defense II (85-7) Off-ball defense including how to handle picks, box out, help out and many defensive situations. 41 minutes

11. Defense III (88-1) Person-to-person, zones, trapping presses half and full court, in-bounds, foul line, center jump and more. 42 minutes

In production 1/1/03

12. Offense I (82-2) Passing technique, all types of passes, plus communication.

13. Offense II (83-0) Moving to ball, faking, communication, timing, and more.

14. Offense III (87-3) The transition game plus foul line, out of bounds, center jump and more.

15. Offense IV (86-5) Offensive setups, plays, and flexible offenses.

More videos to come

Books

A. The Basketball Coach's Bible $24.95 (07-5), 352 pgs; Everything about coaching.
B. The Basketball Player's Bible $19.95 (13-X), 270 pgs; All individual fundamentals.
C. The Basketball Shooting Guide $7.45 (30-X), 45 pgs; Yields permanent improvement.
D. The Basketball Scoring Guide $7.45 (31-8), 47 pgs; Teaches pro moves step-by-step.
E. The Basketball Dribbling Guide $7.45 (32-6), 46 pgs, Anyone can be a good dribbler.
F. The Basketball Defense Guide $7.45 (33-4), 46 pgs, Defense in every situation.
G. The Basketball Pass Cut Catch Guide $7.45 (34-2), 47 pgs, Be an effective team player.
H. Basketball Fundamentals $7.45 (35-0), 46 pgs, Covers all fundamentals.
I. Planning Basketball Practice $7.45 (36-9), 46 pgs, Use time effectively, plan, plus.

Clinics- Check web for current information.
Dates: Usually we run several weekend clinics during the summer.
Cost: The cost is between $50 to $80 per day per person.
Target Audience: The clinics are for coaches and players of all ages. When you work on fundamentals age does not make a difference.

Book & Video Discounts

Check website or call for current discounts:
- 9 book Series (02-4) ~**$20 off**, $78.00
- 2 book Bible Set (20-2) ~**$5 off**, $40.41
- 7 Guide Set (22-9) ~**$5 off**, $46.95
- **10-20% Off** Video 1 with book purchase
- **10-25% Off** 3 or more videos

HOW TO ORDER

Call 800-979-8642,
Fax/phone 215-4358-4459 or use:
mrbasketball.net
Use a credit card, PO (organizations only), check (we hold checks for 10 days) or money order.
Our address:
Golden Aura Publishing, P.O. Box 41012 Phila., PA 19127-1012